GROW

GROW

an awareness journal

Christie Havey Smith

Emerald Shores Publishing
46-E Peninsula Center Dr. #446
Rolling Hills Estates, CA 90274

Printed in the United States of America.
ISBN-13: 9781545631072

*Dedicated to
courageous self-explorers
practicing awareness
at every age.*

INTRODUCTION

Each person's life contains experiences of drifting, putting down roots, opening, releasing, and growing. Like a single seed, we can get lost, but then become determined to find new ground and experience life from a different perspective. There is always an invitation to cycle through a discovery and live more deeply.

No matter where you are in your unique story, this journal is designed to help you nurture your awareness and grow your life. This can be a solo practice saved for your quietest hours, or it can be shared with a trusted group of self-explorers, spurring on mindfulness and understanding.

No matter how you fill these pages or who you share them with, I hope you will not be afraid to crack the binding or spill hot tea on the cover. I hope you will get your favorite pen out of the drawer and let it run free. I hope you will stumble upon new questions and surprising beauty. I hope you will write into your life the very pages you long to write. And I hope you will experience the joy of being the author of your living story, growing wild and free.

– Christie

*May your life be like a wildflower,
growing freely in the beauty and joy
of each day.*

NATIVE AMERICAN PROVERB

CONTENTS

redefining the
DANDELION

CULTIVATE SELF-REFLECTION

Like a seed, become so
gentle that the winds
carry you to a natural
crevice in the earth.
Like a seed, become so
strong that you take root
and rise up to create
new beauty.

*From small beginnings
come great things.*

PROVERB

Here you are in the middle of a page in your story. Who are you?

Awareness Exercise

What positive qualities do you identify with?

How might nature reflect your own human nature?

Creativity	Communication	Compassion	Energy
Spontaneity	Vulnerability	Dreams	Adapting
Full of Light	Feeling	Thoughtful	Intuition

Bright	Fiery	Leader	Intense
Protection	Transformation	Motivation	Passion
Joyful	Determination	Helpfulness	Confidence

Steady	Calm	Honorable	Loyal
Supportive	Grounded	Content	Generous
Dedicated	Kind	Nurturing	Accepting

What part of your true nature might be hiding in the shadows?

What waits to be seen?

*Nobody sees a flower — really — it is
so small it takes time — we haven't
time — and to see takes time,
like to have a friend takes time.*

GEORGIA O'KEEFFE

Come to Light

If you did not fear criticism or challenges, if you felt neither beneath or above anyone, what part of yourself would come to light? Who would you become if you gave yourself permission?

The artists job is to make the invisible, visible.

UNKNOWN

Reflect

What stories have you been told about your childhood? What stories have you been told about your family history? How have these stories impacted your self-understanding?

Renew

What do you believe about yourself, your life?

What aspect of your story might need to be reconsidered or reimagined?

Each morning we are born again. What we do today is what matters most.

BUDDHA

Envision

Take a few minutes to settle into a comfortable seat and close your eyes.
Breathe. Let your mind become a blank canvas. Bring to mind the idea
of growth. What does it look like for you? Is it acceptance? Change?
Forgiveness? Direction or motivation? Confidence or positive thinking?
Is it peace? Perhaps it's something altogether different. What can you
envision for your life?

When you look at a field of dandelions you can either see a hundred weeds or a hundred wishes.

UNKNOWN

Wonder

Return to your innate childlike wonder. Spend a day, an afternoon, or even an hour taking in all that is around you. What do you notice? What do you find amazing?

_____

_____

_____

_____

_____

_____

_____

_____

_____

_____

_____

_____

_____

_____

_____

_____

_____

_____

_____

_____

_____

_____

*Promise me you'll always remember:
you're braver than you believe, and
stronger than you seem, and smarter
than you think.*

A.A. MILNE

Listen

Today take some time to be alone with yourself. No music. No chatter. No cell phone. Just be with yourself. Do something you love to do. Let your thoughts come and then let them go. Listen. What do you hear from yourself? What does your inner dialog sound like? Are you kind to yourself?

Let your inner voice lift from all the other voices. What do you hear?

Raise your words, not voice.
It is rain that grows flowers,
not thunder.

RUMI

You, Redefined

Introduce yourself in the 3rd person.

This is what you would read on the back of your best selling book; it is the first paragraph in your feature article in Vanity Fair; it is the introduction you hear before you walk out on stage and accept your award; it is the thoughtful introduction at the beginning of your biography.

Who are you? Use beautiful words. Give yourself permission to shine.

the
INVITATION

CULTIVATE CREATIVITY

Life is a creative process.

Creativity happens when we connect what is with what could be.

C.H.S.

Awareness Exercise

Sit quietly. Recognize what is taking place within you. If your thoughts, feelings, and sensations emerged as a piece of music, what tenor would it have? What theme?

Passion	Friendship	Growth	Desire
Romance	Imagination	Fear	Family
Hope	Peace	Independence	Healing
Gratitude	Integrity	Beauty	Honesty
Brokenness	Regret	Justice	Anger
Confusion	Generosity	Disappointment	Faith
Discovery	Change	Rebirth	Wisdom
Transformation	Dreams	Gifts	Compassion
Ambition	Forgiveness	Acceptance	Denial
Redemption	Trust	Loss	Possibilities

Where does this music come from?

_____
_____
_____
_____
_____
_____
_____
_____
_____
_____
_____
_____
_____
_____
_____
_____
_____
_____
_____
_____
_____

No matter what music is playing in your life right now, let it be so.

New rhythms and melodies will arise.

*The soul often speaks
through longing.*

SUE MONK KIDD

Name What You Truly Want

The ego may desire control and admiration, but the soul craves personal development, positive impact, and joy. Your soul's desires lead you to become more fully who you are.

What are your soul's desires? Whether they are personal (such as helping a friend or expressing your talents) or universal (such as expanding peace), think big. What if you couldn't fail? Try not to minimize what you want.

Name Where You're Not Free

Ask yourself if you are carrying something into today that belongs to yesterday. Is there an invitation to put it down? To let go, to forgive, to stand up, to change direction? Or perhaps the invitation is to be present to this moment, to its pain and possibility, so that like a seed, you can crack free from your shell.

Is there anything that keeps you from feeling free? Write down or draw what that looks like.

_____

_____

_____

_____

_____

_____

_____

*For a seed to achieve its greatest
expression, it must come completely
undone. The shell cracks, its insides
come out and everything changes.
To someone who doesn't understand
growth, it would look like complete
destruction.*

CYNTHIA OCCELLI

Name Courage

The word courage might make you think of an external show of strength. But often the bravest action is an interior one, an internal shift. It might take courage to let go, to let someone in, or to gather the resilience needed to fully be exactly where you are.

How are you courageous?

Name the Path

What do you dream? What do you hope for? Can you imagine how you might find your way closer to your dreams?

What could you plant today that might bloom tomorrow?

_____

_____

_____

_____

_____

_____

_____

_____

_____

_____

_____

_____

_____

_____

_____

_____

_____

_____

_____

_____

_____

Life isn't about finding yourself.
Life is about creating yourself.

GEORGE BERNARD SHAW

Name the Invitation

Do you feel yourself drawn in a certain direction? Do you feel called to take a leap? What life invitation is awaiting your RSVP?

You're Invited to:

_____

_____

_____

When:

_____

Where:

_____

RSVP:

____ will be there will bells on

____ undecided

Adopt the pace of nature:
her secret is patience.

RALPH WALDO EMERSON

deep
ROOTS

CULTIVATE CONNECTION

When the roots are deep there's no reason to fear the wind.

-Chinese proverb

The question is not what you look at,
but what you see.

HENRY THOREAU

Awareness Exercise

Look around. What do you notice in the world around you? In the
people, the environment, the events taking place? What do you notice
about yourself?

Is there room to look with more gentleness or kindness?

Take a moment to just sit and breathe. As you breathe in, feel yourself fill with warm light. As you exhale, feel yourself releasing heavy thoughts and tension in your body. Spend some time breathing in silence. Imagine yourself filled with color and light. Then make a choice. What lens will you use to see the world?

How might that lens affect the way you see what is taking place right now?

Beauty is the illumination of your soul.

JOHN O'DONOHUE

Connections

A sacred moment is one that illuminates a connection—that reveals your solidarity with others, your preciousness within creation, or that you're linked to the rest of the universe. What are some of your sacred moments?

Love is the flower you've got to let grow.

JOHN LENNON

Love

How would you draw or describe love? Is it a person? A place?
An illusive shape? An action? What does love look like?

How do you embody love?

*Your task is not to seek for love,
but merely to seek and find all the
barriers within yourself that you
have built against it.*

RUMI

A Letter from Love

You know the voice of love. You hear it in the silence. It lives in the oldest room in your heart. What does LOVE have to say to you?

Dear_____,

I have so very much to say to you... _____

_____

_____

_____

_____

_____

_____

_____

_____

_____

_____

_____

_____

_____

_____

_____

_____

_____

Support

Who or what sustains you, supports you, nourishes you?

Deep in their roots,
all flowers keep the light.

THEODORE ROETHKE

The Vital Root

What keeps you rooted in your sense of self?

Root Meditation

Sit comfortably. Breathe deeply, gently. Let your shoulders soften. Let the muscles in your back, your legs, your face, relax. Let your hands rest open.

Feel the ground beneath you, your foundation, strong. With each inhale, feel how the earth holds you, a life growing freely. With each exhale, allow any tentions and anxieties to melt away.

You are cradled by the earth and drawn up by the light. Everything you need to be nourished and to grow springs up from the same earth and is fed by the same light. Everything is as it should be.

Here in this moment, connected to all living things, you are valued and loved.
You are here for a reason.
You are here.
You are.

Sit for a few moments with your eyes closed. With each breath you take, feel how the air that fills your lungs enlivens you. With each exhale, feel how the ground beneath you supports you.

As you open your eyes and return to this moment, notice that you are not blowing through life unattended. You are nourished by the abundant life that is all around.

in the
ROCKS

CULTIVATE WISDOM

There is always
a way through, and
the way begins by
being here.

Awareness Exercise

Take some time to do a self scan. Ask yourself these questions and see what comes.

What do I notice taking place around me?

Do I feel any stress or tension in my body? Can I name where it comes from?

Is there anything on replay in my mind? Worrying me or nagging me?

How is stress impacting me physically? Emotionally? How is it impacting my relationships?

Am I wrestling with any anger or sadness that I need to address? Is there an area of my life where I am stuck or in the dark?

What is my primary emotion?

Can I embrace my life just as it is?

Are there obstacles present in my life? What are they?

Where did the obstacles come from?

Do I feel anything presenting itself to me as possibility?

Where do I feel drawn to grow?

Loving ourselves through the process of owning our story is the bravest thing we'll ever do.

BRENE BROWN

What You Carry

As you begin to become more aware of what a moment offers, you may also become more aware of what you carry with you from one moment to the next. Some of those things may not bring you more fully alive.

Where might you need to open your hands and let go? Perhaps you're holding onto excuses or the need to please others? Maybe you carry criticism, fear, or a past experience that you can't undo? Maybe you harbor negative feelings?

How might releasing something free you to really be in this moment?

*If we really want to love
we must learn how to forgive.*

MOTHER THERESA

Obstacles

Name or draw anything that might stand between you and the experience of presence and joy?

Write down how these obstacles got there and how long they have been around.

_____

_____

_____

_____

_____

_____

_____

_____

_____

_____

_____

_____

_____

_____

_____

_____

_____

_____

_____

_____

_____

Do you, in any way, play a part in the presence of these obstacles?
If so, how?

Nothing ever goes away until it has taught us what we need to know.

PEMA CHODRON

Rocky Terrain Meditation

Sit comfortably. Begin to take slow deep breaths in and out through your nose.

Allow your shoulders to relax and your torso to soften with every exhale.

Find the rhythm of your breath. Allow the breath to breathe you, and bring your awareness into your heart.

Call up an area of your life where an obstacle or a problem is present.

Imagine this obstacle as a stretch of rocky terrain. The sky is dark, and you cannot make out the details of what lies before you.

Seat yourself in this place. Be present to it.

Think about when, where, and how this obstacle began.

Are you alone in this place? Or is there someone else in here with you?

Acknowledge yourself and how you feel. Acknowledge that no one, not even those in this place or ones like it, can speak to your exact experience.

Can you name what you might need to move through this place?

Ask yourself if this is something you already have inside of you?

Call to mind a feeling of being loved.

Call to mind a feeling of experiencing compassion.

As you call to mind feelings of love and compassion, imagine you are now holding a flashlight in your hands. You can now spread a beam of light over the rocky earth.

As you move the beam of light around this space, what is revealed? What details come to light?

Could there be something to find here?

As you move your light over the earth, silently ask the question, what am I meant to discover?

Can this place reveal a gift or an opportunity that has been in hiding? What perspective might there be to gain on your soul's presence here?

Can you change your story, not by changing the circumstances, but by finding a new possibility within your obstacle?

Slowly begin to move your toes, your fingers. Return to this moment.

A New Way of Seeing

Sometimes we have to go into the dark so that we can see ourselves not by where the light shines, but by where it comes from.

What are you being invited to see or discover?

Someone I once loved game me
a box full of darkness.
It took me years to understand
that this, too, was a gift.

MARY OLIVER

Wisdom

When you feel stuck between a rock and a hard place, you might be filling yourself with nuggets of experiential wisdom—gold from the rocky soil. Is there anything of value here to unearth? Could there be a gift in hiding?

*Never let a stumble in the road
be the end of the journey.*

UNKNOWN

Coming Through

Describe yourself as you are today. Have you grown through rocky soil? Use your imagination. Have you navigated craggy roots, dry earth, and grown more hardy? What is beautiful about you now? Are you stronger or more vibrant?

If God said, 'Rumi, pay homage to
everything that has helped you enter
my arms,' there would not be one
experience of my life, not one thought,
not one feeling, not any act,
I would not bow to.

RUMI

Your Most Surprising Thank You Note

If you can name something you're thankful for within an obstacle experience, write it a thank you note.

Dear_____,

Thank you for... _____

_____

_____

_____

_____

_____

_____

_____

_____

_____

_____

_____

_____

_____

_____

_____

_____

_____

_____

_____

unexpected
BLOOMS

CULTIVATE PRESENCE

The surest way to change one's life is not to uproot, but to stay planted long enough to grow the capacity of the heart.

Awareness Exercise

Heliotropism is the directional growth of a plant in response to sunlight. When a flower shifts into the light, it opens, it blooms. As a living thing, how can you adopt heliotropism and turn toward light? Who and what represents the light in your life? What brings about warmth, inspiration, connection, joy, love, meaning? Make a list.

1 _____

_____

2 _____

_____

3 _____

_____

4 _____

_____

5 _____

_____

6 _____

_____

7 _____

_____

8 _____

_____

9 _____

_____

10 _____

_____

There is not one pinnacle in your story, not one bloom on the vine, there will be many. How, in this moment, can you further shift into the presence of light? How can you do the work of opening and grow your capacity to receive and share love and light?

What you'll find when you finally
unclench your fists, fling open
your arms, and with all your courage,
tilt your head back into the sun,
is that your vulnerability is the
most beautiful thing about you.
Bloom wherever you are planted.
Love, like light, will reach you and
grow the capacity of your heart.

C.H.S.

Live Gratefully

What are you grateful for today?

| Unexpected Blooms

Breathe. Your breath is what connects you to this moment.

C.H.S.

See Beauty

At the height of experience you come into contact with yourself.
Name what you see in you.

The answer must be, I think,
that beauty and grace are performed
whether or not we will or sense them.
The least we can do is try to be there.

ANNIE DILLARD

Seek Understanding

What insights are coming forth? Where are you gaining clarity?

Nature is our greatest teacher of transformation. Like water we can dare to flow out and change the shape of things. Or like flowers, we can lift with the light of morning and open.

C.H.S.

Transform

Where there is a shift in your desires, perceptions, or sense of self, there is a transformation taking place. What might that look like for you?

Transformation is always something that happens in the present.
You don't move beyond this moment, you move beyond your form.
How are you taking shape?

You labor to birth something from within. You journey to discover your own freedom. You stumble to pause and find solidarity with others. So you can rise up and change the world.

C.H.S.

Affirm

Try holding this affirmation in your heart:

I have everything I need to love, grow, and prosper. I deserve these gifts and I accept them now.

*It takes courage to grow up
and become who you really are.*

E.E. CUMMINGS

Receive

If you can see the gift of this moment, draw what it looks like. Receive it.

seeds of
JOY

CULTIVATE JOY

There are no ends.
Only new beginnings.
Your life lies before you.
The possibilities are
endless.

*In our consciousness, there are
many negative seeds and also
many positive seeds. The practice
is to avoid watering the negative seeds,
and to identify and water
the positive seeds every day.*

THICH NHAT HANH

Awareness Exercise

Simply witness this moment. Sit in silence and notice what is at work all around you and within you.

What is present that nourishes you or uplifts you? Bow to it or give it a little acknowledgment.

If there is pain, troubles or commotion present, give those things a little bow too.

Offer yourself compassion.

Place your attention on what inspires growth.

Allow for joy.

*Awareness is the
precondition for joy.*

C.H.S.

Practice

When you expand your awareness, you also release anxiety, develop positive emotions, discover present gifts, exercise acceptance, and motivate progress. You grow. How might you further build awareness into your day-to-day life?

Check In

Try checking in with yourself throughout the day with G.R.O.W.T.H.

Get rooted in the moment

Recognize what is taking place

Observe with kindness

Welcome life just as it is

Turn to the light

Harvest awareness

Write it Down

Today I observed... today I realized...

*All the flowers of all the tomorrows
are in the seeds of today.*

INDIAN PROVERB

A Letter to my Future Self:

You will always be growing. What do you want your future self to remember about today. What joy is there to harness?

Dear future self,

There is something important I want to tell you... _____

_____

_____

_____

_____

_____

_____

_____

_____

_____

_____

_____

_____

_____

_____

_____

_____

_____

_____

_____

_____

_____

*Throughout my whole life,
during every minute of it, the world
has been gradually lighting up and
blazing before my eyes until it has
come to surround me, entirely lit up
from within.*

PIERRE TEILARD DE CHARDIN

Experience Belonging

You belong in a field of joy and possibility. This is your time.
You are needed right here, right now. You are enough.

What grows here for you? What grows here because of you?

Dare to Grow

If you have ever seen a lone flower growing in the middle of a dry patch of earth, then you understand how one living thing can completely change its environment. And the loan flower is rarely alone for long. Where life grows, life follows is abundance. Where one seed settles, others sprout and scatter. If you want to change your world, then dare to grow. Right where you are.

What amazing life will you unleash?

*Like a wildflower, grow in places
you never thought possible.*

C.H.S.

Christie Havey Smith, MA, leads awareness retreats and reflective writing workshops in Los Angeles where she lives with her husband and three children.

CHRISTIEHAVEYSMITH.COM